BARRY DAWSON

STREET GRAPHICS
CUBA

with 214 illustrations, 210 in colour

Acknowledgments

For Jenny: invaluable assistant, interpreter, translator, driver and daughter.

Special thanks to Helen Hacker (Düsseldorf, Germany).

PHOTO CREDITS:
p. 34: original Che Guevara photo by Alberto 'Korda' Gutiérrez. © ADAGP, Paris and DACS, London 2001.
p. 35: Che coin by Bernd Wichmann.

Thanks to the following for their support:
England: Jenny Dawson, Grant Devine, Niki Medlik, Fuji UK Ltd. USA: Chris Baker (Cuba and Havana Handbooks, Moon Publications). Cuba: Mario and Yamila, Salvador (Havana), Gustavo (Holguín), Marlon and José (Santiago de Cuba) and of course the numerous Cuban street artists whose work is represented. Germany: Leica Cameras GmbH, Bernd Wichmann. Belgium: Michel.

First published in the United Kingdom in 2001 by Thames & Hudson Ltd, 181A High Holborn, London WC1V 7QX

www.thamesandhudson.com

© 2001 Thames & Hudson Ltd, London.

British Library Cataloguing-in-Publication Data
A catalogue record for this book is available from the British Library

ISBN 0-500-28269-2

Printed in Hong Kong by H & Y Printing

COVER ILLUSTRATIONS:
(Front) Advertising board, page 92; cycle rickshaw, page 50; stamp, page 99; film poster, page 100; propaganda poster; Bacardi drinks mat, page 85.
(Back) Restaurant wall painting, pages 88–89.
Photos by Barry Dawson.

Contents

INTRODUCTION

'The truth that there is such a vigorous Cuba is eloquent enough.'

★ ★ ★ ★ ★ ★ ★ ★

Che Guevara, 1960

The visual street language of Cuba has been dominated by government propaganda since the Popular Revolution of 1959. Hand-painted revolutionary images are a recurrent motif on the island's billboards and murals. In the 1960s, Che Guevara achieved iconic status and his image rapidly came to symbolize populist revolutionary politics and culture. It remains equally popular today, both on government propaganda and tourist souvenirs.

Over four centuries preceding the Revolution, Spanish colonialism, Roman Catholicism, the African slave trade and American capitalism have established an enduring influence on Cuban culture, and its contemporary street imagery reflects this heritage.

Though officially secular, Cuba has two principal faiths, Roman Catholicism and Santería, which are both undergoing a renaissance. Catholic imagery is evident on Cuba's Spanish colonial churches, shrines and in its cemeteries. Santería, the 'rule of saints', is a fusion of Yoruba tribal beliefs and Catholicism, resulting in vibrant imagery interwoven by African slaves and their descendants.

Fifties and sixties design proliferates in Havana. Classic American cars cruise past 1950s hotels nostalgically evoking an era of pre-Revolution tourism and commerce. Original fifties signs and wall paintings fade away in decaying corners of Old Havana. State and public imagery is often rendered in 1960s psychedelic and op art styles, and slabs of fluorescent colour are silkscreen printed on Cuban cinema posters in pop art designs.

The recent reintroduction of private enterprise is mirrored in the appearance of new advertising. An increasing number of signs for accommodation, food and travel services indicate the growth of a de facto dollar economy. Branded consumer goods increasingly bypass the US trade embargo, fulfilling aspirations the Revolution failed to nourish.

The lines between revolutionary socialism and capitalism are blurring around tourism, which has become Cuba's principal hard currency earner. Tourism has stimulated the creative development of indigenous imagery, and street markets heave with clichéd Cuban souvenirs, tailored for the hand luggage of foreign visitors.

The Revolution made Cuba the object of world attention, the focus of a tense political confrontation between opposing superpowers. Surviving almost

half a century of radical change, Cuba now faces the supreme challenge to its ideological survival: a free market economy. Its street imagery is moving gradually from propaganda towards persuasion.

Street graphics are transient, with change often being imperceptible until seen retrospectively. This book represents a subjective view of that ephemeral process in the year 2000. These photographs are a record of Cuban street imagery at a defining moment in the country's history.

REVOLUTION

'The duty of every revolutionary is revolution.'

★ ★ ★ ★ ★ ★ ★ ★

Fidel Castro, 1959

AUTENTICOS!
REPRESENTANTES

Miguel
ALFONSO POZO
CLAVELITO

José
PIÑEIRO PAEZ

BECERRA *Senador*

GRAU PRESIDENTE

opposite and below Election campaign placards, Old Havana, 1950. Note the prominent Coca-Cola sign, and to its left, a partially obscured advertisement for 'Hatuey' beer. The anti-capitalist single-party politics of today ensure that only the Cuban Hatuey beer ads remain on the walls of post-Revolution Cuba.

left An original 1950s campaign placard from pre-Revolution political elections, on sale in Havana's market.

SU VIDA TENDRA GARANTIA
CON ANTONIO EN LA ALCALDIA

ANTONIO ALCALDE

1950

Destruction of the Plaza
Casino, Havana, in January
1959. Casinos and nightclubs
were viewed as symbols of
Western decadence and
became early targets of
revolutionary fervour.
Havana's fabled casinos were
run by American organized
crime and supported by
Cuba's former military
dictator General Batista.

left and above The cover and centre pages of 'Revolución Cubana 1952–1959', an album of collectable picture cards documenting the Revolution and its leaders.

Pre- and early Revolution ephemera increasingly appears for sale in the street markets in Old Havana's Plaza de Armas.

TRIUNFO
DE LA REVOLUCION
CAIDA DE BATISTA

244.—Madrugada del 31 de Dic. de 1958, Batista es informado en Columbia por los jefes de su ejército, de las grandes derrotas sufridas. Cunde el pánico.

245.—Convencido de su derrota, el sátrapa renuncia y huye cobardemente hacia Santo Domingo, con varios familiares y adictos.

246.—Cantillo asume el mando del Ejército y convoca a varios civiles, tratando de formar un nuevo Gobierno, con el Dr. Piedra como Presidente.

247.—Al enterarse Fidel de lo ocurrido, declara no aceptar ningún Golpe de Estado y ordena a Guevara y Cienfuegos marchen sobre la Habana.

248.—En la mañana del 1 de Enero, al conocer el pueblo la huída del tirano, se lanza a las calles lleno de júbilo, frenético de ansias de libertad.

249.—Al grito de: "¡Muera Batista y Viva la Libertad!" el pueblo, en formidable avalancha, entra en el Castillo del Príncipe y libera a los presos.

250.—Los muchachos del 26 de Julio, con ametralladoras, les guardan la retirada. Afuera, los familiares les esperan. Reina la alegría. Estallan besos y abrazos.

251.—20 soldados y 20 policías no se atreven a disparar. Por las laderas del Castillo suben amenazantes los familiares y el pueblo, enardecidos.

'Triumph of the Revolution – the Fall of Batista', the concluding spread from 'Revolución Cubana', a set of 268 marginally out-of-register four-colour picture cards, which were originally free with 'Felices' canned fruit (1960–61).

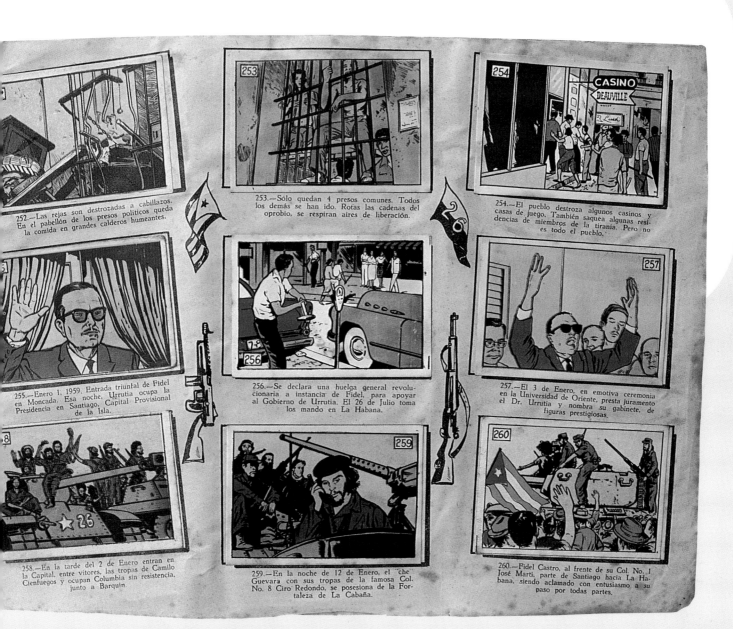

252.—Las rejas son destrozadas a cabillazos. En el pabellón de los presos políticos queda la comida en grandes calderos humeantes.

253.—Sólo quedan 4 presos comunes. Todos los demás se han ido. Rotas las cadenas del oprobio, se respiran aires de liberación.

254.—El pueblo destroza algunos casinos y casas de juego. También saquea algunas residencias de miembros de la tiranía. Pero no es todo el pueblo.

255.—Enero 1, 1959. Entrada triunfal de Fidel en Moncada. Esa noche, Urrutia ocupa la Presidencia en Santiago, Capital Provisional de la Isla.

256.—Se declara una huelga general revolucionaria a instancia de Fidel, para apoyar al Gobierno de Urrutia. El 26 de Julio toma los mando en La Habana.

257.—El 3 de Enero, en emotiva ceremonia en la Universidad de Oriente, presta juramento el Dr. Urrutia y nombra su gabinete, de figuras prestigiosas.

258.—En la tarde del 2 de Enero entran en la Capital, entre vítores, las tropas de Camilo Cienfuegos y ocupan Columbia sin resistencia, junto a Barquín.

259.—En la noche de 12 de Enero, el "che" Guevara con sus tropas de la famosa Col. No. 8 Ciro Redondo, se posesiona de la Fortaleza de La Cabaña.

260.—Fidel Castro, al frente de su Col. No. 1 José Martí, parte de Santiago hacia La Habana, siendo aclamado con entusiasmo a su paso por todas partes.

above 'ANTIMPERIALISTAS', a fading slogan in the decaying centre of Old Havana. Sweeping public statements about Cuba's enemies seem to be declining as foreign tourism becomes the country's principal industry.

The party newspaper 'Revolución' (1959–61) was renamed 'Granma' after the 20-seat passenger boat that brought the first group of 82 revolutionaries from Mexico in 1956. The original American owner of the boat had named it in honour of his grandmother.

below 'Viva Cuba Libre' – a popular slogan in Old Havana and throughout the country.

CUBA
CORREOS 1976
1
XX Aniversario del Granma

below and right **Slogans in Santa Clara province.**

★ ★ ★ ★ ★ ★ ★ ★ ★ ★ ★ ★ ★ ★ ★

right A giant cut-out figure of Fidel Castro on the Havana to Trinidad road. There are surprisingly few representations of Castro in Cuba's streets. Popular icons such as Che Guevara and Camilo Cienfuegos, who achieved mythical status through death, are the images chosen to symbolize the party's political identity.

Camilo Cienfuegos was a commander in the original group of 82 guerrillas who instigated the Revolution in 1956. He died in a plane crash off the Cuban coast in 1960.

The image of Cienfuegos, bearded and with long hair as he entered Havana after thirty months of guerrilla warfare, promotes the principles of revolution. The iconic popularity of Camilo Cienfuegos on Cuba's propaganda canvas is only exceeded by that of Che Guevara.

SEGUROS DE LA ★

25

Postage stamps are foreign
ambassadors for Cuba's political
and cultural identity. Numerous
anniversaries communicate
poignant moments in the island's
history to an international audience.
The early wars of Independence
and Soviet achievements in space
are depicted in a distinctive graphic
style on these Cuban stamps.

JAMAS DEFRAUDAREMOS LA SANGRE derramada.

¡VIVA CUBA LIBRE!

LA HISTORIA NO TIENE MARCHA ATRAS

Conceived in the mid 1850s, the Cuban flag was adopted as national emblem when Cuba became a republic in 1901.

The white stripes symbolize purity and the blue stripes stand for Cuba's original three departments. The single white star represents Cuban independence, and its red ground the blood of its martyrs. There is a heavily stylized use of the national flag throughout all fields of Cuban graphics and it remains a classic international emblem of revolution.

left A triumphal steel arch crowned with the Cuban star of independence pays tribute to leading educationalists outside the university in Pinar del Río. The Revolution's vigorous education programme brought mass literacy to Cuba.

above A relief portrait of Cuban revolutionary hero Abel Santamaría, cast in concrete, which seems to float on a fountain of water. Santiago de Cuba.

above An anomaly of post-Revolution Cuba. Guantánamo province at the eastern tip of Cuba became the site of a US naval base in 1901, and remains so today on a 99-year lease agreed in 1934.

right A comment on US–Cuba relations inscribed in a concrete footpath. Vedado district, Havana.

above Posters demanding the return of six-year-old Cuban boy Elián González, rescued from the Florida Straits and taken to the USA. 'Elián has become the greatest symbol for Castro's Cuba since Che Guevara', commented the *New York Times* on the ensuing political fallout.

right A citizen of Havana wears a T-shirt featuring the most widely accepted of Cuba's three official currencies.

*'In April 1966 a very large picture of Che Guevara
was painted in colors on the wall of the bus terminal
for routes 60 and 65 in El Cerro, Havana.'*

★ ★ ★ ★ ★ ★ ★ ★ ★ ★ ★ ★ ★

Declassified CIA report, 1966

opposite No other icon is as universally recognizable as the messianic 'Guerrillero Heróico' image of Che Guevara. The portrait, shown here in full frame, was shot with a Leica M2 camera by Cuban photographer Alberto 'Korda' Gutiérrez in 1960.

Countless derivations of Korda's image flow through the streets of Cuba. Banknotes, coins, stamps, souvenirs, billboards and murals on government and private buildings all feature the Heroic Guerrilla image.

Korda's iconic portrait remained unpublished until 1967. En route to Milan from South America, Italian publisher Giangiacomo Feltrinelli was aware of Guevara's probable execution in Bolivia for guerrilla activities. A stopover in Havana resulted in Korda giving Feltrinelli a print of his picture.

Within days, Guevara was dead. Within hours, Feltrinelli published a poster. Within months, an estimated two million copies were sold. Korda's image of Guevara became the emblem of an era, crucial to the bedroom walls and street demonstrations of a student generation. The image remains present throughout Cuba.

right Guevara as a tropical landscape, a painting for the tourist market on sale in Havana's Plaza de Armas.

FABRICA DE
CHOCOLATE
INAUGURADA POR EL CHE
EL 1º DE ABRIL DE 1963

left Che's chocolate factory, inaugurated by Guevara as Minister for Industry, two years after he left the presidency of the National Bank of Cuba.

above The Ministry of the Interior building, Cuba's political nerve centre in Havana's Plaza de Revolución. This portrait of Guevara in steel, glass and neon is illuminated during rallies in the square.

Argentinian born, Dr Ernesto Che ' Guevara de la Serna was described in 1965 by Jean-Paul Sartre as 'the most complete man of his age'. In 1995, Guevara's grandson recalled his mother's words about Guevara: 'He was never home.' Che Guevara was executed in 1967 by government soldiers in Bolivia, entering history and the FBI's largest file as the ultimate revolutionary. He became a 20th-century icon. The legend and image of Guevara are a national asset, exploited to meet the tourist demand for books, T-shirts, posters and a range of dubious souvenirs.

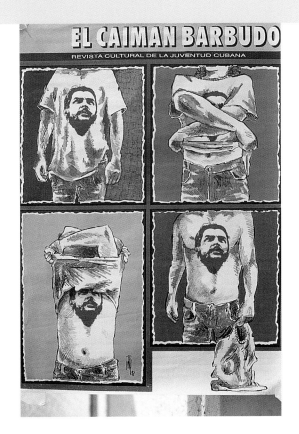

EL CAIMAN BARBUDO

REVISTA CULTURAL DE LA JUVENTUD CUBANA

Che , comandante , amigo

CUBA

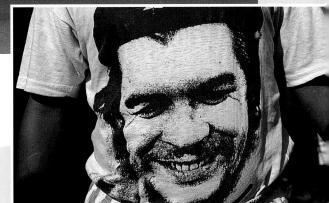

TRANSPORT

Classic American cars of the 1950s cruise the streets of Havana. Original classic car parts are finite, and many cars sport an eclectic trim. Parts may be simply missing or reassembled incorrectly. Midnight Auto Parts is a thriving business, and cars are closely guarded.

below left One of Cuba's two rare 1959 Mercurys, in front of the capital's Teatro de la Habana.

below right Chevrolet's collectable 'Hot One': a 1957 V8 Bel Air, now a taxi for tourists visiting Havana's Capitolio Nacional. This one has additional winged insignia from a 1956 model.

opposite above Front fenders from a range of famous 1950s manufacturers: De Soto, Studebaker, Plymouth and Pontiac.

'No Aleida, the car belongs to the government, it is not mine and you cannot take advantage of it. Take the bus like everybody else.'

★ ★ ★ ★ ★ ★ ★ ★ ★ ★ ★

Che Guevara to Mrs Guevara on transport for shopping, 1963

above **Tail details of a 1957 Chevrolet Impala** (left) **and Soviet Lada** (right).

Fender to fender: classic 1950s Chevrolets
parked in Havana's Parque Central.

'Bici Taxis' are Cuban cycle rickshaws. Their owners paint designs on the passenger seats, basing them around names, zodiac signs or statements of love and desire. Santa Clara province.

Havana's taxis range from unrecognizable wrecks, through to nostalgic classics and an increasing number of shiny Japanese imports. Cruising past the revolutionary slogans are vehicles born from limited resources and unlimited inventiveness, such as this Lada stretch limo.

ACCIDENTES 5

MUERTOS 1

LESIONADOS 4

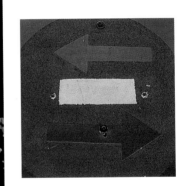

left Road signs are almost non-existent in Cuba. The few visible are often vague or contradictory, and accidents are not uncommon.

above A park sign prohibiting popular pleasures in Santiago de Cuba.

'The use of bicycles is an indication of cultural progress', said a 1990 editorial in *Bohemia* during the 'Special Period' of fuel rationing. Thousands of imported Chinese bicycles were given to citizens who earned merit through work.

below and opposite above Hand-painted child safety signs on the rear of buses, in the faded colours of 1950s Cuba.

opposite below Cuba's lack of traffic and economic difficulties make road maintenance a low priority. The major road hazard is the road itself. The unfinished Russian-built Autopista is officially an eight-lane highway, often without divider lines. It is frequently reduced to only four or two lanes, with the occasional large mound of earth circumnavigated by a dirt track.

★

I N D U S T R Y

'There is a crisis in production.'

★ ★ ★ ★ ★ ★ ★

Che Guevara, 14 August 1962

'There is no crisis in production.'

★ ★ ★ ★ ★ ★ ★

Fidel Castro, 14 August 1962

The crisis in production of the 1960s was eased when the Soviet Union replaced the USA as principal sugar crop buyer. However, the Soviet demise of the 1990s left Cuba facing serious economic problems and an austere rationing programme known as the 'Special Period'. Today, salvation comes from an unexpected source: tourism. The Cuban cigar industry is well represented in the booming arts and craft markets of Varadero, Cuba's main holiday resort.

opposite above **Partagás cigar factory, Havana.**

left **An old cigar box insert on sale in the Plaza de Armas book market, Havana.**

above and right **Paintings frequently feature cigar smokers. These are by local artists in the street galleries of Baracoa, Guantánamo province, eastern Cuba.**

Waste leaf from the major cigar brands is used in Cuban cigarette production.

GRAN FABRICA DE TABACOS

MANLY

JOSE JIMENEZ PEREZ-HABANA

Old printed cigar box inserts and decorative cigar bands with embossed gold leaf work are on sale to foreign collectors in Havana's Plaza de Armas book market.

Tobacco is grown in the fertile landscape of Pinar del Río, Cuba's westernmost province. Famous brands include Romeo y Julieta, Monte Cristo and Castro's own favourite before he stopped smoking, the coveted Cohiba.

Byron

HABANA

THE BIGGEST ATTRACTION IN VARADERO

UNDERWATER VIEWER VARASUB I

AY WINDOW CABIN.
CONDITIONING.
CITY: 48 PASSENGERS.
ILY DEPARTURES FROM
ART-PARADISO-
ENA RESORT.
N-OUT.

stands
tourism
els and
atives

00 USD. *
0 USD. *

t previous notice *

above 150 km (95 miles) north-east of Havana lies Varadero, a beach resort developed for lucrative foreign tourism. Until recently, Varadero's major attraction was sex tourism. Now, government curbs and Western investment are combining to encourage more family-orientated values.

right and opposite Souvenirs of Cuba on sale in Varadero market include cane work, ceramics and recycled drink cans. The unofficial presence of Coca-Cola bypasses the US trade embargo via Mexico.

Domestic industries and agriculture feature on hand-painted billboards along the roads of Cuba's thirteen provinces. Many of these use cut-out imagery.

HOTELS
RESTAURANTS
BARS

'*Mi Mojito en La Bodeguita, mi Daiquirí en El Floridita.*'

★ ★ ★ ★ ★ ★ ★ ★ ★ ★ ★ ★

Ernest Hemingway, 1954

Cuba's most famous American resident, author Ernest Hemingway, made two bars and a hotel into drinking landmarks and shrines for visiting fans. When Hemingway lived in Old Havana's Hotel Ambos Mundos during the 1930s, La Bodeguita and El Floridita were his favourite bars. His scribbled quote is enshrined in La Bodeguita del Medio amidst the graffiti that covers the bar inside and out, inscribed by every literary tourist with a marker pen or Swiss Army knife.

above The marble patio of the 1930 Hotel Nacional features the motif of Cuba inside a compass, pointing north across the Florida Straits towards Miami.

left The landmark twin towers of Havana's Hotel Nacional reflected in a 1957 Chevrolet Impala taxi.

above The colonial-style Hotel Imperial in Santiago.

right The Hotel Inglaterra was built in the late 19th century. Once popular with writers and artists, its most notable patron was Federico García Lorca. Situated on Havana's Parque Central, its refurbished colonial style attracts tourists who in turn attract taxi drivers with classic cars, including this 1956 Chevrolet Bel Air, the legendary 'Hot One'.

left and below *Casas particulares* and *Paladares* (places of taste) are a new commercial phenomenon: officially licensed private homes which provide accommodation and food, respectively, to foreign visitors.

above Tourism in 1950s Havana was controlled by
American Mafia boss Meyer Lansky from the rooftop
swimming pool of the Hotel Capri, still a stylish locale.

right New nightclubs, bars and restaurants are opening
in Varadero and Havana.

The famous Tropicana open-air night club. Errol Flynn, Nat King Cole, Frank Sinatra and Marilyn Monroe were among the guests and entertainers at Havana's 'Paradise under the Stars'.

La Zaragozana, Old Havana.

'Culture brings freedom.'

★ ★ ★ ★ ★ ★ ★ ★ ★

José Martí, 1891

Pre-Revolution Bacardi drinks mats and trademark promotional items are common in the markets of Havana. Bacardi established rum production as a major industry in Cuba's second largest city, Santiago de Cuba, in 1862. After the Revolution they departed, taking their name, recipe and famous bat logo to Puerto Rico.

CAFÉ TABER

The Caney rum factory, Bacardi's old premises, still
produces export-quality rums, including Havana Club.
Its trademark is a representation of 'La Giraldilla',
a bronze statue from Havana's 16th-century fortress,
the Castillo de la Real Fuerza.

right A restaurant wall
painting in Holguín.

far right A humorous
sign for pork
sandwiches, outside
a Santa Clara café.

below A pizza place in
Santa Clara, with the
surreal logo of a man
holding a boot.

CASA de las EMPANADAS

Horario 7.00 am 7.00 pm

Coppelita $1°

Signs from snack bars and ice cream vendors in various parts of the country.

Tome Coca-Cola Deliciosa y Refrescante

above A pre-Revolution enamel Coke sign.

left 'Bread is the fountain of life': this street vendor's cart in Santiago de Cuba illustrates another major feature of Cuban life: queuing for staple items.

right A fading soft drink ad from the 1950s in Old Havana.

below A pre-Revolution Hatuey beer mat and a contemporary bottle label feature the head of 16th-century Cuban Indian chief Hatuey.

93

Street murals are the main evidence of painting in Cuba, but local artists also line the tourist paths of Old Havana and Baracoa with their canvases.

A popular theme is the humour and pathos of Cuban life, depicted in brightly coloured paintings and ceramics with a strong Cubist influence.

*'Fidel Castro is not indifferent to the arts —
it would be better if he were.'*

★ ★ ★ ★ ★ ★ ★ ★ ★

Gabriel Infante, 1991

Film is in the vanguard
of the Cuban arts. Movies
are popular and every
city has many cinemas.
Cine 23 y 12 is in the
Vedado district of Havana.
Foreign collectors seek
out movie memorabilia
in Havana's markets.

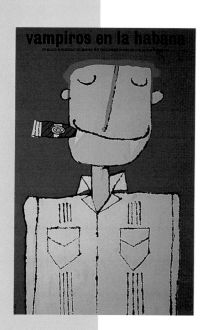

Cuba has developed a creative, intelligent film industry with talented Cuban directors. Tomás Gutiérrez Alea first achieved fame for *Death of a Bureaucrat* in 1966, and in 1993 received international acclaim for *Fresa y Chocolate* (*Strawberry and Chocolate*) which explored gay issues in Cuba. The use of silkscreen-printed cinema posters dates from the 1960s.

ASI BAILABA CUBA

beny moré

SILVIO RODRÍGUEZ
CAUSAS Y AZARES

odeon

MIGUELITO VALDÉS
MÚSICOS CUBANOS FAMOSOS

75 Cuba
RITA MONTANER
MÚSICOS CUBANOS FAMOSOS
CORREOS 1999

LAS RAICES
DE LA SALSA
Documental Cubano
Director: Sergio Nuñez

'Son' is the traditional music of Cuba, a rural fusion of Spanish melody and African rhythm. 'Salsa' was developed from Son by New York Cuban-American jazz musicians in the 1950s. Now both forms enjoy international success.

Music needs no promotion in Cuba: it is everywhere, all the time. Music imagery is seen in street sales of old records, on stamps, tourist souvenirs and the instruments, bandstands and collection boxes of street musicians.

RELIGION

Puedo esperar
mas que lu
porque soy el
tiempo

Salvador
26-10-95

'It is illegal and punishable to oppose the Revolution
with religious faith or belief.'

★ ★ ★ ★ ★ ★ ★ ★ ★ ★ ★ ★ ★ ★

Cuban constitution, article 54, 1976

Callejón de Hamel in Havana is a centre of Santería worship. Local artist Salvador González has transformed the street into a vibrant celebration of the religion through his paintings of symbols and images that represent its practices and beliefs.

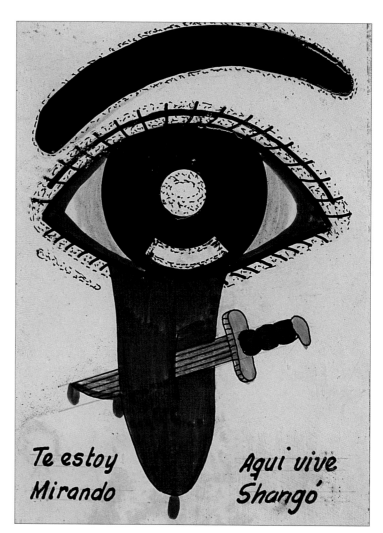

Santería is a fusion of Catholic and African beliefs developed by Cuba's African slaves and their descendants. The name itself means 'the rule of Saints'. Images of Lazarus rising from the dead, a protective eye to warn off evil spirits, and cockerels and their blood are all common symbols.

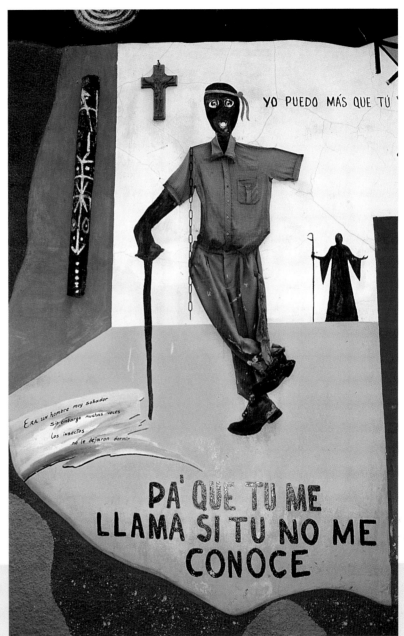

FIEL HASTA DESPUES DE MUERTA
RINTI

above and right Cuba's main Catholic cemetery is the Necrópolis
Cristobal Colón (Christopher Columbus). A Madonna and Child
sculpted in Carrara marble, a stained glass headstone and a
sleeping dog with its English mistress carved in granite can
all be found in Havana's city of the dead.

opposite A derelict church in Trinidad.

opposite, top left A tattooed sugar cane cutter.

opposite, top right A Catholic shrine on the Cuban roadside.

This popular Catholic image of the Virgin Mary protecting fishermen from a storm is found in many graveyards and shrines. Here it appears on a pre-Revolution advertisement for 'Mejoral' headache remedy.

OBSEQUIO DE

Mejoral

contra **DOLOR** de **CABEZA** y **RESFRIADOS**